The Story of NACHIKETA

How A Little Boy Conquered Death By Meditating On A Force Superior To Death

Sri Vishwanath

www.soulpowermagic.com

First Printed in the United States by
Vervante.

ISBN: 978-0-9817703-5-2

www.soulpowermagic.com

**You can contact the author at
vish@vish-writer.com. You
can also reach him at his US number at
2138142680.**

Also by Sri Vishwanath

1) **The Joy of Becoming God**
2) **Shakti** : Revealed- How You Can Feel Great In Sixty Seconds Flat
3) **Zero Effort** : How To Achieve Big Breakthroughs In Your Life In Less Than 30 days Flat
4) **Know" That One Thing"** - The Spiritual Guide That Been 5500 years in the making. Discover The Quickest and surest path to God...
5) **Shraddha**- Everything You Wanted To Know Above Love And God
6) **No-Nonsense Meditation –** What The Greatest Wise Men & Women Knew About Human Consciousness That You Are Not Aware Of.
7) **Shiva** : The story of How God Mentored An Ordinary Man To Experience Extraordinary Levels of Super Consciousness In A Single Game Of Dice.
8) **Give Up --- Everything That You Love.** 24 Simple Mind Exercises That Great Men & Women Effectively Use Every Single Day

Dedication

TO LORD KRISHNA, SRI RAMAKRISHNA,
SWAMI VIVEKANANDA & Sharada Devi

How A Little Boy Conquered Death By Meditating On A Force Superior To Death

****

Nature does not manifest her laws bit by bit, an inch of gravitation today and another inch tomorrow. No, every law is complete. There is no evolution in law at all. It is given once and for ever. There may be a thousand laws and we may know only a few today. We discover them- that is all.

Swami Vivekananda

****

Vajashrava, a pious sage, lived 5000 years ago at a sacred place on the banks of the Yamuna River in Southern India. The seer had a son named Nachiketa who was sharp, witty, talented and extremely intelligent. It was a natural practice by the sages of those days to give away all their prized possessions to poor people in order to attain the divine grace of God. One day Vajashrava decided to sacrifice everything that he possessed and loved dearly. He called all the poor people and gifted them with his cows. Nachiketa was watching everything that his father was doing. His father was giving away all the cows which were old and yielding no milk. How could his father attain the blessings of God and secure a place in heaven by offering cows whose skins were barely hanging on their bony frames, whose udders weren't giving milk, and whose teeth could hardly chew?

Nachiketa approached his father and told him that what he was doing wasn't right. He reminded his father that he had to sacrifice everything that he loved, not everything that he didn't want.

Father, I know you love me the most. To whom will you offer me to? Nachiketa asked.

Vajashrava didn't pay attention to his son's words and told him to go and play. But Nachiketa was insistent.

Father, why don't you offer me to God and get his blessings and secure a place in heaven?

Nachiketa kept pestering his father for an answer. After a while Vajashrava became irritated and angrily retorted. *Alright, Nachiketa I offer you To Death.*

And so it was. What Vajashrava spoke became a reality.

Nachiketa found himself in the chamber of death. The lord of death was Yama. He was the first man to die and he later on became the lord of death. It so happened that Yama was away for three days and so Nachiketa was waiting outside his chamber eager to meet the lord of death. On his return Yama was told by his attendants that a young boy has been waiting outside his chamber for the last three days without food and water.

Yama greeted Nachiketa and was highly pleased with the little boy's courage and curiosity to meet him.

Nachiketa, your time for death has still not arrived. My attendants will take you back to where you came from.

However, before they do that I want to gift you with three boons for the three days you spent outside my chamber without food and water. Ask whatever you want and I, the lord of death, will fulfill your wish.

Little Nachiketa was thrilled. *The first thing I desire, O Lord of Death, is that my father shouldn't be angry with me and he should be able to recognize me and not think about me as a ghost who has returned back from the kingdom of death.*

Your wish is my command and so will it be, Yama promised. *Seeing you freed from the jaws of death, your father will get over his anger and love you more dearly. This I assure you, Nachiketa Now ask me the second boon that you desire.*

O, Lord of Death, I.ve heard from my father and many other wise souls about a sacrificial fire which when performed rightly grants one a place in heaven. Enlighten me on the right way of performing this great sacrificial fire.

Yama, highly pleased with the little child's curiosity to know the subtle aspects of the sacrificial fire, went on to explain in detail the exact process of conducting the fire sacrifice which leads one to heaven.

From today this sacrificial fire will be named after you, Yama promised. *It will be called the Nachiketa fire sacrifice. Now ask me the last boon that you desire.*

Nachiketa thought a moment. *This doubt that arises consequent on the death of a human being – some saying 'It exists' and others saying 'It does not exist' --- I would like to know this clearly under your instruction, O Lord of Death. This is my last and most wanted boon.*

Yama,, no longer smiling and jovial, suddenly turned serious.

With regards to your question as to what happens to a human being after death this is a doubt even the gods entertained, Nachiketa. Death, being a very subtle matter, can't be truly expressed. Ask me some other boon; do not press me for this boon.

But Nachiketa was determined. *O, Lord of Death, if even the gods had doubts over this matter and if you yourself the King of Death feels that it can't be comprehended, there is no other boon comparable to this one. I can't think of any other better instructor than you to clear this doubt, so please grant me this boon, mighty one!*

Yama shook his head. *Ask for sons and grandsons that will live a hundred years. Ask for animals, elephants, gold and a vast expanse of the earth. And you yourself to live as many years as you like, but give up this boon you demand. Ask for all those things that are desirable by human beings but difficult to get - abundant wealth, long and healthy life, beautiful and loving women, intelligent and respecting children, unlimited power on earth like no human being has ever enjoyed. All these pleasures and power I grant to you, Nachiketa but don't inquire about death anymore.*

Nachiketa, though tempted by this marvelous opportunity to experience some of the most desirable aspects on earth, remained still like a vast lake – perfectly quiet and completely serene. Then he said: *O, lord of death, great and rare as these pleasures are they waste away the vigor and spirit of every human being. I don't desire all these things which are ephemeral in nature. Let all these things go to others. Grant me that wisdom to the other world. This is the only boon I seek.*

Yama was unhappy with this response, but Nachiketa continued.

No human being on earth was ever satisfied with the wealth he owned.

No human being has escaped pain and suffering on earth. There is no pleasure without pain. I don't entertain any of these transcendental delights. Having met you, O Lord of death, I know that I will be always wealthy. Having come in contact with you I know that I will continue to live a long, healthy and peaceful life. But the boon that is worth praying for is knowledge about what happens after death, knowing which one can attain immortality. With respect, O Lord of Death, this is my only remaining desire.

Yama, having tested Nachiketa thoroughly and finding him fit for the highest knowledge, now spoke thus:

I'm pleased with your sincerity and boldness, Nachiketa to enquire about "that one thing" which even the most intelligent people avoid in pursuit of personal passions. Your curiosity and sacrifice to give up everything for this priceless knowledge is noteworthy. I've never revealed the secret of what happens after death before to anyone, but I'll reveal it to you. Listen carefully.

Yama explained to Nachiketa that what dies with death isn't worthy to be mourned. That which doesn't die with death is worth paying attention to.

The Mother of All Sources

So the moral of this fable is that destruction is nothing but going back to its source. But what is this source to which it goes back?

Consider an example.

Can you think about the sun if the word "sun" didn't exist?

There are three important things in the above question

a) The gross external object – the sun
b) Thought - about the sun
c) The word - "sun"

Notice that you can't think about the sun if the word "sun' never existed. This means that there is a connection between the thought, word, and the gross object.

You can't perceive the external world of objects without thoughts and you can't think without words. The word

has to exist first before the thought. A word is made up of sounds. It follows then that the sound is the beginning of all creation. Sounds become words and words become thoughts and thoughts manifest into external objects.

Consider this other example.

Can you think about a car if the word "car" didn't exist?

The car is the gross object which would never have come into being if the idea about developing a car never existed. This idea is nothing but a subtle intelligence which is represented in the form of a thought. We have seen earlier that thoughts are made up of words and words have to exist first before a thought manifests. The idea about developing a car has its root in a sound which then takes the form of a word which eventually evolves into a thought, thereby facilitating the manifestation of the car in its gross form.

Everything that exists in this world in a gross form has its root in a sound which is nothing but its subtle intelligence. The sun, moon, stars, trees, animals, plants, human beings, air, water, fire, earth - everything in this universe couldn't have been created **if the idea of that object of creation hadn't existed**. This idea or subtle intelligence has its origin in a sound which gradually evolved into a word and then into a thought and finally into an external object. **Sound is the beginning and source of all creation.**

The Source of All Creation

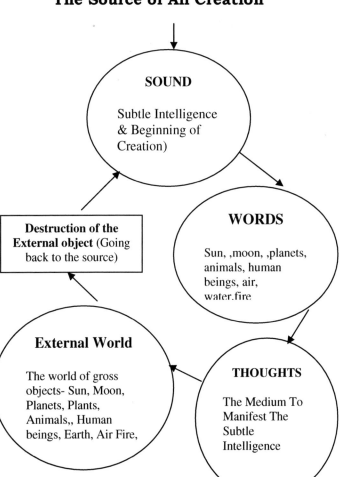

SOUND

Subtle Intelligence & Beginning of Creation)

WORDS

Sun, ,moon, ,planets, animals, human beings, air, water.fire

Destruction of the External object (Going back to the source)

THOUGHTS

The Medium To Manifest The Subtle Intelligence

External World

The world of gross objects- Sun, Moon, Planets, Plants, Animals,, Human beings, Earth, Air Fire,

The Sound Symbol

Nachiketa, the Lord of Death continued his instruction, *I'll now reveal to you the mother of all sounds. By meditating on this primal sound you will gain the supreme knowledge of "that one thing" which doesn't die with death. This sound is the first manifestation from 'that one thing' and it pervades every single object in the universe. This sound is the best representation of every other combination of sound. It evolves through the correct pronunciation of the three letters A- U- M. When pronounced correctly it sounds as OM....OM... OM.*

Nachiketa listened intently as Yama went on.

Anyone who meditates on this sound OM... formed through the combination of these three letters (A-U-M) acquires knowledge of 'that one thing' which is the source of all creation and into which all things return back after they die. This combination of letters is the best sound symbol out of which the whole universe manifested. Take the letter A. It's pronounced without touching any part of the tongue or the palate. It's the root sound and represents the beginning of the whole sound process.

Nachiketa nodded, taking in everything told to him.

When you pronounce the letter U it rolls from the very root to the end of the sounding board of the mouth. The letter U represents progress of the whole sound process. M is the last sound in the series and can be produced only by closing the lips. The letter M represents the end or dissolution of the sound process. Thus the sound Om... (A-U-M) represents the whole phenomenon of sound-producing and is considered the matrix of all sounds.

I see, Nachiketa said.

Yama nodded, satisfied with the youth's attention. ***It should be noted that OM is a sound and it hasn't any relationship to any language****. It's simply a sound. By meditating anyone can gain knowledge of this whole process of creation, progress, and destruction of the universe. The sound OM (A-u-m) is the only sound which when pronounced rightly activates every single nerve center in our body. No other combination of sounds helps to achieve this desired result. So meditate on this great sound of Om. When uttered with complete sincerity, devotion, and love it will help you cut through the ignorance of* *the thinking mind and bring you in contact with your real nature, your true divinity.*

Now Yama gave Nachiketa more time to reflect on all that he had been told.

The Power Of OM Found in All Religions

O Arjuna, I am the taste of pure water, and the light of the moon and sun. I am the essential nature of the mantra Om mentioned in the holy scriptures, the sound in ether, as well as the courage and the virility of human beings.

Krishna to Arjun in Bhagavad Gita

When I read the Bhagavad-Gita and reflect about how God created this universe everything else seems so superfluous.

Albert Einstein

In the beginning was the Word and the Word was with God and the Word was God. Amen. (AUM)

Amen, which basically means, "so be it", is widely mentioned in the Bible. It is used during worship to confirm an oath or that one agrees to moral laws. The word amen has in many ways evolved out of the word AUM.

Bible St. John 1:1

A few centuries after Christ amen was adopted into Islam as Amin or Alm. The Arabic letter "l" is pronounced like "u" when it appears before a consonant which means that Alm automatically becomes Aum.

Om is an integral part of the philosophies, rituals, meditations and chants in Jainism, Sikhism and Buddhism.

It is said that all the teachings of the Buddha are contained in the sacred verse: "*Om Mani Padme Hum.*"

Note that the English word "omnipresent" which means "present everywhere" starts with "om."

Yama, seeing Nachiketa ready for more instruction, continued to mentor the enthusiastic youth. *Nachiketa I'lll now reveal that aspect within you that doesn't die with death.*

Nachiketa waited patiently.

Everything that exists in this universe is an act of creation, which is nothing but manifestation of something which already exists. The sun, the moon, the stars, the planets, animals, plants, human beings and everything that we call the universe already existed in a fine form This act of manifestation of the universe from this fine form is called prakarti (cosmic intelligence) The first evolution of this cosmic intelligence was sound which denotes a source. Imagine you're walking in the street and someone calls you by your name. You immediately turn in the direction of the sound. Sound denotes a source. This source is nothing but space - the whole universe. Everything that fills the space between the sky and the earth. This space which sound filled in manifested into ether or matter.

Nachiketa nodded with understanding, his eyes gleaming with his new knowledge.

Further imagine that having located the source of the sound while walking in the street you now turn in the direction the sound. Someone touches you from behind,

Sound gradually evolved into touch *and from touch manifested the element air.*

I understand," Nachiketa said.

What happens after someone touches you from behind? Yama asked and then answered himself. *The person reveals himself to you. You are able to see and identify the person.* **Touch evolved into form** *and from form manifested the planet Sun which gave rise to the element fire.*

What do you do next after a person reveals his identity? You strike a conversation with him if necessary. You get to know him better – his likes and dislikes – his tastes. **Form evolved into taste** *and from taste manifested the element water. Once you get associated with the person and get to know him better, what you do next?*

You bond with him. **Taste further evolved into smell** *and from smell manifested the element earth*

Yama waited a few moments for Nachiketa to digest everything, and then he continued.

Thus earth, water, fire, air and space - the

five elements of nature -evolved out of the five sensations of smell, taste, form, touch and sound.

*These five sensations of sound, touch, form, taste and smell gradually evolved into the "I consciousness". Consciousness means awareness associated with sound, touch, form taste and smell. **This consciousness had three properties associated with it**. The first is called the Tamasic guna (property) which means awareness related to the association with the five objects of sensations. Thus the five human organs of nose, tongue, eyes, skin and ears which are related to the sensation of smell, taste, sight, touch and sound evolved out of the tamasic nature of the 'I consciousness'.*

The second property of the 'I consciousness' is called Rajasic guna which means awareness related to the association with instruments of action and knowledge. From the skin evolved the instruments of action- First the hands manifested and from them came the faculty of strength; then the feet manifested and from them came movement; then the generative organs manifested and from them came the ability to reproduce. Blood vessels manifested and from them evolved the stomach and from it arose hunger and thirst. Then the heart manifested and out of it evolved the instrument of knowledge- the intellect.

The third property of the I consciousness' and the most important property is called Sattvic guna - the ability to rise beyond the mind and the body awareness and associate oneself with the ultimate source – the cosmic intelligence. In this state of awareness your daily activities are guided by the power to discriminate between the real and the unreal – between knowledge and ignorance. You don't get dejected when faced with grave danger, nor overcome by delusion at the sight of attractive things. You don't feel proud when your personal goals are achieved and you're not affected by the criticism of others. You retain the mind and body consciousness but you gain this wonderful ability to take mental flight. From the sattvic guna evolved the instrument of divinity- Chitta (the pure cosmic mind.

Nachiketa continued to digest all this material, his mind swelling with the burst of knowledge he was getting.

The pure cosmic mind is simply the ability to recognize the source of all intelligence from which everything manifests. It's a characteristic of the 'I consciousness' and shouldn't be confused with the intellect. **The intellect is associated with the power of reasoning while the chitta is associated with inspiration. Inspiration doesn't contradict reason; it rather fulfils it.** *It's a higher level of awareness of one's consciousness. (Krishna, Christ, Buddha, Mohammed and all the great inspirational men and women had the Sattvic guna completely manifested in them.)*

The sun, moon, planets, ocean, mountains, plant life, animal kingdom all evolved out of the first two properties of the 'I consciousness' - the tamasic and rajasic guna. Notice at least one of these qualities in all of nature and animal life – the sensation of sound, touch, form, taste, smell or the instrument of action.. It's only in human beings that you will find all the three qualities manifested – The tamasic, the rajasic and the sattvic – the bodily, the mind and the divine.

Rest now a while, Yama said. *Let all this knowledge sink in.*

Diagram Of Sound's Properties

This diagram should help illustrate the properties of sound.

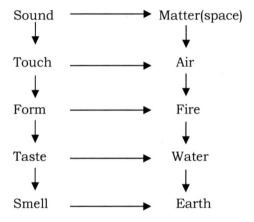

How The Universe Evolved Out of Prakarti

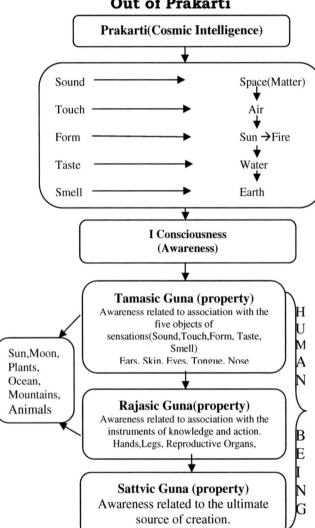

Both rested, Yama now resumed imparting great secrets to his pupil.

Nachiketa, I'll now reveal how time was born and why understanding time will help you understand life after death.

Prakarti (the cosmic intelligence) had manifested everything it possibly could. Space, air, fire, water, earth, ocean, rivers, mountains, planets, plants, animals and human beings. It had all the aspects of the universe fully manifested. But there was a big problem. All these aspects of the universe remained separate, incapable of coming together to form and run the world.

(As a digression, imagine a team of the most talented technical people in the world to come together and develop 10 of the fastest computers in the world. These computers are capable of processing the most voluminous data in lightening speed. Imagine further that a company wants to buy all these 10 computers and put them to use in their business. However, before buying them they wanted each of these 10 computers to be able to communicate with each other. Therein lay the problem. The team which developed the individual computers lacked the intelligence to make these computers communicate with one other. The point being: **The intelligence required to bestow unity is many times superior than the intelligence which grants individuality**.

Prakarti or the cosmic intelligence could only bestow individuality on every object of the universe, Yama went on. *It lacked the intelligence to bestow unity. That intelligence which bequeaths unity, that oneness is called Purusha (God or soul) When that intelligence entered into Prakarti (the cosmic intelligence) the universe came into being.*

Then to Nachiketa's great surprise Yama related a poem.

O Nachiketa the moon's soft light, the stars so bright,
The glorious orb of the day, He shines in them,
His beauty might- reflected lights are they.
The majestic morning, the melting evening,
The boundless billowy sea,
In nature's beauty, songs of birds,
You will see through them- It is He.

Thou speakest in the mother's lay,
That shuts the babies eye
When innocent children laugh and play
You will see Thee standing by.

When holy friendship shakes the hand,
He stands between them too,
He pours the nectar in mothers kiss
And the babies sweet 'mama'
Thou wert my God with prophets old,
All creeds do come from Thee,
The Vedas, The Bible and Koran bold
Sing Thee in harmony.

'Thou art', 'Thou art' the Soul of souls
In the rushing stream of life.
'Om Tat Sat Om' Thou art my God..
My love, I am Thine, I am Thine.

****

This Purusha. Nachiketa, is the highest form of intelligence which pervades the whole universe. There is no force superior to it. It's the fuel to the cosmic intelligence, the force which keeps this universe ticking. Being superior to all other intelligence it can't be acted upon by any other force. It enjoys an independent and absolute existence, incapable of being destroyed. It is eternal and timeless.

I understand, *Nachiketa immediately said, wanting to show Yama that his instruction wasn't being wasted on one so young as himself..*

This Purusha is without beginning and end though it appears to have a beginning and end when seen through the aspect of Prakarti. Time, which is a characteristic of Purusha, creates this delusion in our minds that the universe had a beginning and that the universe will have an end. However, this isn't true. Time isn't linear but cyclical. All of creation follows a cycle. Take a seed, it grows into a plant and eventually into a gigantic tree. And then it dies leaving only the seed. It completes the circle- it comes out of the seed, becomes the tree and then ends an the seed again. Take the raindrop drawn in the form of vapour from the ocean, then changed into water and finally converted into vapour again. Take the huge mountains. They're continuously being worked upon by glaciers and rivers which are slowly but surely pounding them into sand. This sand then drifts away into the ocean where it settles down on its bed layer after layer, becoming hard as rocks once more to be heaped into mountains of a future generation. Again they will be pounded and pulverized and the course goes on. From the sand will rise these mountains and unto sand they go and so on. Take animal life. Look at the bird, and how it springs from the egg, lives its life, and then dies, leaving other seeds of future birds. As with animals, so with human life.

A cycle, Nachiketa acknowledged.

Yama nodded. *The word beginning, Nachiketa, simply means the beginning of a cycle of creation. It nowhere means the beginning of the whole cosmos. It's impossible that creation could have a beginning. It only appears to have a beginning through the aspect of time mounted on nature. Whereever the word beginning of creation is mentioned it means the beginning of a cycle of creation. In every cycle of creation there's a beginning and an end. The end is the cause for the new beginning and the beginning is the cause for a new end.*

Understand what a cycle of creation means. There was a time when everything was dark. The sun didn't exist, nor the air, sky, water, or human life – nothing existed. There was no life and there was no death. There was no night or day.

(As another digression, Milton in his great poem *Paradise Lost* explains this phenomenon as "No light but darkness visible." Kalidasa, the Indian poet, explains it as "Darkness which can be penetrated with a needle.)

Yama studied the youth he was mentoring and was satisfied of his attention and comprehension.

It was gloom hidden in gloom. Everything was parching and sizzling. The whole creation seemed to be burning away for days when one afternoon a speck of cloud arose in one corner of the horizon. In less than half an hour it had extended over the whole earth until it was covered with cloud. Then the clouds released a tremendous deluge of rain. The cause of creation was described as will. The Purusha which existed at first had become changed into will and this will manifested itself as desire- the cosmic intelligence (Prakarti).... and the whole of creation began.

Everything that has a beginning must have an end. ***Everything that is created is subject to change and must undergo the greatest change of death or destruction.*** *This whole universe which was created has to undergo the biggest change of destruction. This destruction is nothing but going back to the source- the*

Purusha. The sun, the moon, the stars, the plants, animal life, and human beings - everything has to go back to its source. Nothing is spared under the law of time. This creation and destruction of the universe is called one life cycle of the universe.

Nachiketa, I'll enlighten you now on how one life cycle of the universe is calculated and what happens at the end of a cycle of creation.

The sun is the source of all energy, all life which sustains this universe. Everything in this world including the earth and all the planets receive their light and source of strength from the Sun. The Sun is the center of the whole solar system and its life is 4.32 billion years. At the end of its life span of 4.32 billion years the entire universe is destroyed and it goes back to its source.

The intelligence which governs the aspect of time is called Brahma and one life cycle of the universe makes up one unit of Brahma. This one unit is called kalpa. One kalpa is 4.32 billion years.

Time has two aspects- the real and the apparent. *That which is real is based on* *the consciousness of time and that which is apparent is based on the practical applicability and division of time. That which is real is timeless and that which is apparent is limited. Purusha when it entered into Prakarti took the form of a jiva which stands for the individual soul present in every living being. Out of Jiva manifested the Prana (the life force) which is the key to human consciousness. Human breathing which evolved out of Prana is the real aspect of time. It's the fly wheel of the whole system of human consciousness. Breathing first acts upon the lungs, the lungs upon the heart, the heart acts upon the blood circulation, this in turn acts on the brain and the brain on the mind which produces the awareness of the outside world. **Time therefore begins with human breathing, the act of inhalation and exhalation which makes us aware of all existence.***

Understand, Nachiketa, that breathing isn't restricted to the act of inhaling and exhaling. Instead, it's the ultimate medium through which the body unites with the soul. Prana- the life force causes the motion of the breath through two currents which passes through the brain and circulates down the sides of the spine, crossing at the base and returning to the brain. These two currents are the called Pingala (the sun current) and the Ida (the moon current). The first one, Pingala the sun current, starts from the left hemisphere of the brain, crosses at the base of the brain to the right side of the spine, and recrosses at the base of the spine like one half of the figure eight. The other current Ida (the moon current) reverses this action by starting at the right hemisphere of the brain and completes this figure eight. These two currents are responsible for all the mind and body functions in our system. These currents flow day and night and make deposits of the great life forces at different points in our body; but most human beings are rarely conscious of them and fail to direct these divine forces to supercharge their consciousness.

Breathing is intimately connected with these two currents. The science of breathing gives a new direction to the 'sun' and 'moon' currents. It opens for them a new passage through the center of the spinal cord. This transformation is achieved through the technique of Raja yoga. Yoga means union, that which unites or yokes the body to the soul. The center of the spinal cord contains a very fine brilliant thread called Sushumna which is luminous and can be felt and seen through constant practice and concentration. This thread which begins from the base of the spine and ends at the pineal gland is the seat of all spiritual and divine power that you see manifested in any human being. That technique of breathing is the basis of supreme consciousness. **Time therefore begins with human breathing which makes us aware of all existence, both bodily and divine**.

I'll now reveal those aspects of time intimately connected with breathing and which forms part of one life cycle of the universe. One prana (act of breathing) is equal to four seconds which is the time taken to pronounce 10 long syllables.

Know that 720 such respirations make up one muhurta which is equal to 48 minutes. Muhurta is a special aspect of time which deals with the science of performing the right actions at the right time. **Time isn't so much about time management as it is about understanding the science and art of perfect timing**. Time is about performing the right actions at the right time. Three things are needed to succeed in any great venture: concentration, perseverance, and the will of god. This will of god is called the secret of perfect time.

Knowledge, human effort and perseverance can only take you so far; but it's the art of perfect timing that transcends all barriers and brings in the big results. So understand that time is all about perfect timing.

Look around and you'll notice that behind every great success are two things--- perfect positioning and perfect timing. The former is related to human intellect and the latter to the art and science of time. Starting a new business venture, forming long term associations, administering medicines for curing grave illness, entering into a new house, buying and selling property, performing holy activities, entering into new relationships- all succeed when you begin it at the right time. Think about how many times you asked for something from your loved one, parents or employer and you didn't get it. You asked at the wrong time and so you didn't succeed. If you had asked at the right time there was a good chance for success.

Understand furthermore, Nachiketa, that the science of time shouldn't be confused with the science of astrology- The science of time deals specifically with the art of performing the right actions at the right time.

Note that 30 such muhurtas of 48 minutes each make up one day of 24 hours, the time taken by earth to complete one full rotation around its own axis. **A day does not begin with dawn and end with dusk.** A day begins with one sunrise and ends with the next sunrise. Each day is divided into 30 muhurtas which is further divided into four equal parts of 7 ½ muhurtas each. The period from sunrise to noon, noon to sunset, sunset to midnight and midnight to sunrise is each made up of 7 ½ muhurtas.

The best time in a day is the 29th muhurta (the second to last muhurta before sunrise). This time begins 96 minutes before sunrise and lasts for 48 minutes. Leaders throughout history have acknowledged this aspect of time and meditated in this holy hour. Those who meditate on the word A-U-M during these 48 minutes will make swift and rapid progress in their spiritual life; they will be gifted with special ideas to help them overcome major obstacles and manifest their true dreams. This muhurta, called the Brahma muhurta, is considered the most auspicious time to connect with the core of your being.

These are great things to know, Nachiketa marveled.

A month doesn't begin on the first and end on the thirtieth Yama nodded. *The term month is derived from the word 'moon_eth'. Each month begins on a new moon and ends with the next new moon. Each month is made up of 29.5 days which is the time taken by the moon to complete one full lunar cycle starting from new moon to full moon to the next new moon. Each day of the month is characterized by the various phases of the moon in relation to the sun. This aspect of time is called Tithi – the time it takes for the longitudinal angle of the sun and moon to increase by 12%. There are 30 Tithis in a month, each of them having a certain characteristic which influences the thinking patterns of individuals.*

Moon, Nachiketa, is the embodied aspect of human mind and influences many important human activities. *The study of the various phases of the moon (waxing and waning) and its influence on human life is called Tithi. A month is made up of 30 tithis. Each tithi contains many secrets for performing the important and daily activities of life at the right time.*

Twelve such months of 29.5 days each make up one solar year of 354 days. Since the earth takes 365 days to complete one full circle around the sun every 2 ½ years one extra month of 28 days is added to fix days in relation to the sun. The 12 months are based on the entrance of the sun into a zodiac sign.

Understand, Nachiketa, that the two major motions of earth will help you understand the signs of the zodiac and the apparent path which the sun takes through the sky.

The earth has two major motions- the rotational motion around its own axis and its orbital motion around the sun. The first one is the reason why you see the sun move from the east to the west every day. The sun doesn't move from the east to the west but it appears to move because of the earth moving around its own axis.

The second motion of the earth is the orbital motion around the sun. The earth takes 365 days to complete one orbit around the Sun. Thus, the average speed is nearly one degree per day (360/365). Since the sun is much nearer than the stars, this orbital motion makes the sun apparently move among the stars.

Actually, this motion of the sun is due to the Earth's orbital motion around the sun, and while doing so, the sun apparently moves through different stars, depending on Earth's place in its orbit.

This apparent path among the stars during this orbit is represented by a line in the sky called the Ecliptic; and the stars through which the sun passes through in this line are called the signs of the zodiac. These constellations or stars are 12 in number and further sub-divided into 27 luminous bodies called Nakshatra. Together, these stars and nakshatras represent and influence the qualities and characteristics of human nature.

This apparent motion of the sun across the sky where it passes through these 12 constellations and nakshatras together with the study of Tithi (phases of moon) and muhurta form the science of perfect timing which is called Panchang.

So 360 solar years make up a divine year and 12, 000 such divine years make up one maha-yuga (sub-cycle) = 4320000 solar years. The 4.32 million solar years is sub-divided into four eras of human existence characterized by the element of good and evil present during those periods.

The first period is called Satya Yuga -- the golden age where virtue, knowledge, honesty and love abounds. Every living being is blessed with abundance and there is peace and happiness. This period lasts for 1,728,000 solar years.

The second period is called Treta yuga where there is a slight decline in virtue and wicked activities slowly creeps in. This age is marked by 75% virtue and 25 % vice activities. This period lasts for 1,296,000 solar years.

The third period is called Dwapara yuga where there is a marked decline in virtue. This age is characterized by 50% virtue and 50% vice activities. This period lasts for 864,000 solar years.

The fourth and the last period is called Kali yuga where wickedness, cheating, and immoral activities will be at its peak. The purest of men and women will be severely tested and face big obstacles while wicked people will roam freely. This age, characterised by 90% vice and 10% virtue, will lasts for 432, 000 solar years.

Note, Nachiketa, that we're currently going through this last period of Kali yuga which began on 18th February 3102 BC. So 5112 years have elapsed and 426, 888 years remain.

One thousand such maha-yugas of 4.32 million years make up one unit of Brahma which is 4.32 billion years. At the end of 4.32 billion Years, which is one unit of Brahma, the universe will be destroyed as the sun will cease to exist and life will come to an end.

However, Nachiketa, the idea of the universe which existed at the time of destruction shall become the cause of creation for the next cycle of creation and so on.

- -

(Here are values to help readers understand the elements of life cycles. One life cycle of the universe = 4.32 billion years (the age of the sun).

One prana (respiration) = four seconds
One muhurta = 720 prana =48 minutes
30 muhurta = 24 hours
One month = 30 days
One solar year = 360 days(corrected every 2 ½ years)
One divine year =360 solar years
One maha yuga = 12000 divine years = 4.32 million solar years

One kalpa (unit of Brahma = 1000 maha yugas) = 4.32 billion years= age of the sun.

Note that the age of the sun calculated by modern science is around 4.57 billion years which comes close to what Hindu sages found out 5000 years ago without the use of current technology. Current scientific research does support the existence of occasional mass extinctions in earth's history. These include the following major extinctions.

a) Ordovician/Silurian extinction event about 440 million years ago
b) Devonian extinction event about 375 million years ago
c) Triassic extinction event about 250 million years ago.

Though these dates of mass extinctions differ from 4.32 billion years it gives sufficient proof and insights into the concept of creation and destruction of a cycle of the universe.)
****

Seeing that Nachiketa was still alert and closely following his words, Yama went on.

Truth isn't about seeing and believing, Nachiketa. It's about being and becoming. Truth is about acknowledging the real aspect in you- the Purusha and striving to realize that Purusha in you. The highest reward for the greatest action performed is an intense experience which purifies one's mind and makes one fit for the utmost knowledge - love for the Purusha.

Understand, Nachiketa, that time isn't arbitrary. It has a deep significance in relation to the performance of right actions at the right time. Human consciousness begins with breathing but doesn't end with death. When the heart beat stops the body dies but human consciousness continues to exist in a subtle form in the Jiva (the individual soul). The seat of the Jiva is in the mind. The mind, though an inseparable part of the human body, enjoys an independent existence through the aspect of Jiva; it doesn't die with the body.

(As a modern comparison, data in a computer has an independent existence and is capable of being transferred from one computer to another computer without dying when the computer is destroyed.)

Time can only put an end to things which are created. *Everything that is created without exception will get destroyed with time. Your body was created with the intelligence of your mind and so when the heart beat stops the body dies. Your mind was also created but the intelligence which created your mind is a superior intelligence and this intelligence forces your mind to exist when the body dies and retains your consciousness through the aspect of Jiva.* ***This intelligence which sustains the mind and which doesn't die with the death of your body is called Karma.*** *Karma and Time are two aspects of the Purusha (God or soul of unity) which runs this whole universe through the existence of Jiva (individual soul) present in every being.*

Karma simply means the need for intense experiences generated by the mind during a life time which remains unfulfilled at the end of a life span. Every thought that you think makes an impression in your mind. The nature of your thought determines the impact of the impression made in your mind. Routine activities like the act of brushing your teeth, eating food, taking a bath don't make deep impressions in your mind. **However certain thoughts can create major impressions in your mind and facilitate the need for the mind to seek a suitable experience to fulfill it.**

Now I understand Karma, Nachiketa said.

All the deep impressions which remain unfulfilled at the end of a life time will become the cause for Karma to find suitable bodies to re-enter and work out these relevant experiences. When the mind no longer feels the need to work out more deep experiences Karma releases the mind from the task of finding more bodies and the mind goes back to its source- the purusha.

(Consider an example. You go to work. You meet various people during the day. On your way back to home you see a pretty woman and you're greatly attracted. Before you go to sleep you recollect the events of the day and the only image which comes before your eyes is the vision of the beautiful woman. You can't help it. That image has formed a deep impression on your mind and forces you to keep thinking of it. You get up in the morning and that image still hasn't left you. You can't ignore these deep impressions formed in your mind and these impressions force you to think and act in a particular way unless you can counteract that impression with a much stronger impression.)

Understand, Nachiketa, that the mind has an independent existence in the form of deep impressions and these profound impressions represent the mind and become the cause for its continued existence. During a life time a number of deep impressions make their way into our mind. You might have a very close and intimate relationship with your parents, brothers, sisters, children, wife, friends, or with animals. Your attachment to your loved ones would be so deep that it would have an independent existence of its own and become the cause for a fresh, more meaningful and deeper experience with them in your future lives.

Similarly, one might have a dream of becoming a multi-millionaire, or flying in space, or becoming a painter or whatever it is that one wants. Every human being has desires and dreams whose strength gives them an independent existence. They become the cause for a more meaningful and deeper experience in our future lives.

Nachiketa, I'll now enlighten you on those

seemingly apparent contrasts in child birth and human personalities which will help you understand the law of karma. Why is it that one child is born to a poor family and suffers with hunger while another child is born in a wealthy kingdom and enjoys the best of luxury? Why one child is born pure and becomes God-like while another acquires wicked characteristics and becomes a terrorist? Why two brothers born and raised in identical conditions grow up to become two completely different personalities - one giving up the world by becoming a monk and another enjoying the world by becoming a director of a company?

The answer which logic and reasoning can provide to these questions falls short of the expectations of the highest mind. So listen carefully as the intelligence of Karma answers these subtle questions.

Every child is born with a fund of experiences which are simply the deep impressions which the mind has accumulated over a series of life times. No child comes into this world with a blank slate.

And I was no different, Nachiketa murmured.

True, Yama agreed, as another rest period ensued.

To better understand Yama's explanation, consider this example:

You're walking along the street and you see a dog. How do you know it's a dog? Understand how your mind functions to arrive at the conclusion that it's a dog.

1) The moment you see the dog there's a *mental impression* of the dog formed in your mind.
2) Your mind then searches for *similar group of impressions* of the dog already existing within the mind.
3) When your mind locates similar group of impressions of the dog already existing in your mind it's satisfied that it's a dog. This process is what is called as *knowledge*. You now know it's a dog.

4) If your mind is unable to locate similar group of impressions of the dog already existing in your mind it won't be satisfied and this process leads to *ignorance*.

Knowledge is a process where your mind *refers* your present experiences to a group of previous experiences already stored within your mind in the form of impressions. If your mind is successful in finding a group of previous experiences similar to that of the present experience it's satisfied and this whole process is considered knowledge. If it isn't successful, it's referred to as ignorance.

The significance of this process means that it's impossible to attain knowledge without a fund or group of previous experiences already existing in our mind.

This discovery opens up an interesting aspect of human life. Notice that the power of acquiring knowledge varies substantially in each individual. How is that possible? It must be that the child has come with a fund of knowledge. It just can't be otherwise. Every child born in this world comes with a fund of knowledge and experiences. He or she doesn't come with a blank slate. If the child comes with a blank slate it's impossible for the child to attain any level of intellectual power, because he or she wouldn't have anything to refer to.

How the Mind Functions

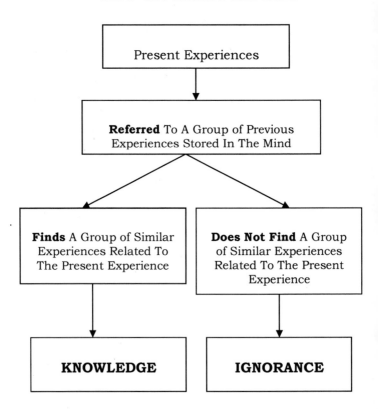

Mozart wrote a sonata when he was four years old and an opera in his eighth year. Theresa Milanolla played the violin with such skill that many people thought that she must have played it before her birth. Pascal, when twelve years old, succeeded in discovering the greater part of geometry. The shepherd Mangiamelo, when five years old, calculated like an arithmetical machine. Adi Shankaracharya, the great commentator of the Vedanta philosophy, finished his opus when he was twelve years old.

Zerah Colburn, when he was eight, could solve the most complex mathematical problems instantly and without using any figures. The list goes on. How could such accomplishments be possible at such tender ages? From where did these personalities get all their knowledge and ability?

The world considers these skills as a gift of talent. But what is talent? It is nothing but knowledge and there is only one way of getting knowledge - through experience. There's no other way out. But if we haven't had knowledge - creating experiences in this life - we must have had these experiences in other life times.

Consider another example:

A little child wants to buy a pair of shoes. He's on the lookout for a particular design of the kind of shoe which he likes. He goes into the shopping mall with a parent and finds dozens of stores which sells shoes. He walks into the first store but doesn't find the design he's looking for. He goes into the second store with the same result. At the third store he finds the exact shoe he desires. He wears the shoe, finds it comfortable, and his parent makes the purchase. The child is happy as they leave the store.

Now pick the best answer from the two choices below:

1) The little child got the shoe because of the third store in the shopping mall.

2) The little child had a desire to buy a particular design of the shoe which led him to the third store in the shopping mall where he found the right shoes.

Which of the two choices above is the best explanation for the little child finding the right shoes?

Without a doubt it's the second explanation given above. It was the desire of the child to buy a particular design of the shoe which led him to the store where he found the right shoes. If this is true then why do we say that "The child exists because of the parents." Wouldn't it be better if we say "The child had a bunch of desires to fulfill which led him to the right parents who gave him birth."

Parents aren't the real reason for the child coming into existence, just like the store isn't the real reason for the child finding his right shoes. Parents are there only to provide the best environment for the child to grow. It's children who select their parents and not the other way round.

It's the most insane idea that the child comes into existence solely because of the parents. We make a big mistake of not recognizing the identity of the child in this whole process. Children carry with them an identity in the form of the fund of experiences which leads them to select the right parents and which, in due course, becomes the cause for their future growth.

Swami Vivekananda wrote:

The men of mighty will the world has produced have all been tremendous workers- gigantic souls with wills powerful enough to overturn worlds, wills they got by persistent work through ages and ages. Such a gigantic will as that of a Buddha or a Jesus could not be obtained in one life, for we know who their fathers were. It is not known that their fathers ever spoke a word for the good of mankind. Millions and millions of carpenters like Joseph had gone, millions are still living. Millions and millions of petty kings like Buddha's father had been in the world. If it was only a case of hereditary transmission, how do you account for this petty prince who was not, perhaps, obeyed by his own servants, producing this son whom half a world worships? How do you explain the gulf between the carpenter and his son whom millions of human beings worship as God? It cannot be solved by the theory of hereditary. The gigantic wills which Buddha and Jesus threw over the world, whence did it come? Whence came this accumulation of power? It must have been there through ages and ages, continually growing bigger and bigger until it burst on the society in a Buddha or a Jesus even rolling down to the present day? All this is determined by the law of karma"

Now Yama decided it was time to continue Nachiketa's education.

The law of karma, Nachiketa, says that no one can get anything unless he or she earns it. *One of the aspects of Karma is the law of cause and effect. Every action that you perform either expands your consciousness or contracts your consciousness. When you generate wealth for yourself and your family you feel happy and your consciousness expands. When you distribute a certain portion of your wealth for charitable purpose you feel great and your consciousness grows wider. When you love your partner and your children your consciousness develops. When you extend this love and affection to everyone that you meet your consciousness enlarges further.*

Conversely, when you continue to hate someone who has caused you harm your consciousness contracts. When you waste your energy (life force) in routine repetitive talks which don't help you to evolve into a better being your consciousness narrows. When you spend more time in the world of thinking and less in the world of spirit (by acknowledging your true nature-the Purusha) your consciousness lessens.

This expansion and contraction of consciousness produced by voluntary actions gives rise to the law of cause and effect. During our daily life we ignorantly project the desires of our little self (thinking mind) over the Jiva (individual soul) and cause our consciousness to expand and contract. This mistake on our part of not conducting our daily activities in line with the real nature of Jiva makes us fall into the cycle of karma- the never ending cycle of cause and effect. One cause leads to another effect which in turn leads to another cause and so on.

*Nachiketa, He who sees the Supreme Lord(Purusha) dwelling in all beings alike, the imperishable in the things that perish, he sees indeed for seeing the lord as the same present everywhere **he does not destroy the self by the self** and goes on to achieve the highest goal.*

Think about it. How many times in the past have you destroyed the self (soul present in others) by the self (soul present in you)? How many times have you hurt others by putting someone down or cursing someone for prolonged periods? How many occasions in the past have you taken advantage of someone in a relationship? How often have you taken liberty of a person's ignorance to accomplish your personal interests? Look what you are doing. You're attempting to destroy one soul through another. We're ignorant of our real nature and so our actions produce effects which keep coming back on us. The pain that we send out to the world comes back to us much stronger at a later point of time to hurt our own consciousness.

Time creates this ignorance in us, making us believe any pain and suffering we feel is undeserved. However, that isn't true.

All the pain and suffering was our own creation but with the passage of time we forgot to remember its true identity and when it struck back on us we couldn't understand the reason and the cause. **There's no effect without a cause just as there's no pain and suffering without a relevant conscious action.**

Time through the happening of events only makes it appear to you that you've been denied the fruits of your action. This is, however, not true. Look around and you'll notice unworthy people occupying prime positions of power. Undeserving people enjoying wealth, luxury and fame. Hardworking and honest people struggling in their daily life. People of integrity being questioned and put to test.

How could all this happen, Nachiketa? How can an unworthy person become worthy of occupying a position of power? How can an undeserving person become qualified to enjoy the pleasures of life? How can a straight forward person be made to walk the path of pain and suffering reserved for the crooked and wicked people?

Understand, Nachiketa, that which you see with your eyes and perceive with your mind is only the current personality of the person. **The current personality of a person isn't the real cause for the current effects or circumstances in the individual's life.**

Take the case of an unworthy person occupying a prime position of power. What you see before you is the unworthy person and you immediately come to the conclusion that this person isn't fit for this coveted position and got it by inadequate reasons. What you don't understand is this *big secret. – No one can get anything unless he or she earns it. If that position is a coveted or worthy then it should be that at some point of time that person produced pure actions which made him or her worthy for that role in the future.*

The world attempts to link the current personality of the person to the current circumstances. And when they can't find a relevant match they call it luck or destiny.

*This is however not true, Nachiketa. There's no force in the world which can escape the law of karma- the law of cause and effect. **Just as good karma which the unworthy person had once produced brought him to be placed in that coveted position, so also the bad karma which the unworthy person is now creating in his or her current position will become the cause for the individual's decline in the future**. Time creates this illusion that events happen by chance but that isn't true- every event is well deserved and can be clearly understood if only one had the capacity and the will to unite the right cause to the right effect.*

(Here, in a digression, is another example. Two men go to watch a movie. The first man enters the movie hall before the start of the picture while the second person enters the theater only after the first interval. The second person finds the hero thrashing the villain in the second half of the movie and isn't able to figure out why the criminal was being hit so badly for no fault of his. The first man who had watched the movie from the beginning never had these doubts for he saw clearly the underlying cause which produced the bad treatment meted out to the villain.)

So don't worry, Nachiketa, about all the events and people which put you down. Don't worry about the way the world treats you. March ahead with the supreme knowledge that there's no power in the world which can stop the fruits of a good karma to reach you. No such power existed before and no such power will exist in the future. What you do is yours. Both the good and the bad. You can choose to let go of the bad by firming up the good, and you can choose to expand the good by conducting your daily activities in line with your soul. The choice is yours. The power of the whole universe is waiting with open arms to embrace you, encourage you, and give you that extra inspiration to live the life you're meant for. Your current circumstances don't represent you. They only represent your current thinking. You're not your thoughts but a point of light that can dazzle this whole universe.

Understand, Nachiketa, there's nothing to grieve over for all the pain and suffering which one is enduring. Take responsibility and know for certain that just as bad karma creates bad effects good karma creates good effects; and these good effects not only mitigate those past harmful causes but also pave the way for love, light and joy to enter into your life.

Raise the self by the self and keep creating good karma, Nachiketa. This is what every great soul aspires to.

Now you should understand what good karma means. Any action of yours which causes the least injury to others and maximum good to the world is what you should strive for. There's no action in this world which is completely pure or which doesn't cause injury to others.

When you breathe thousands of microbes die. When you read a holy book in the night by turning on the light thousands of micro beings are killed by that ray of light. So no action in this world is free of injury just as there is no fire without smoke. Take up actions which reflect your personality and in the process try to do the best for the world through the core of your being.

Every human being starts with Pravartti (I consciousness). So place yourself at the center of everything and conduct your daily activities to the best of your abilities. Make yourself happy, make your family happy and as you progress in this direction move your little self away from the center. Expand your consciousness. That which you are seeking is already yours. That which you love in your near and dear ones manifests from the core of your being.

*Meditate on this great truth. The brilliance of Purusha- the intelligence of unity which pervades in every other being. Break free from the patterns of putting your-self before your idea. Try to feel the pain of the world as yours. Experience the joy of the world as yours. Meditate on the sound of A-U-M from which everything manifested. Feel the vibration within. Keep moving your little self away from the center of all your actions. This aspect of our consciousness where our little self dissolves into the ocean of Purusha (the God of unity) is called Nivritti. **The gradual movement of***

moving your little self from the center of all your actions and allowing it to be led by the consciousness of unity (the Purusha) is the greatest aspect of karma and it's achieved through the law of non-attachment.

Realize that the law of non-attachment releases you from the law of cause and effect. Listen to this story which will help you understand the law of non-attachment.

One day, a young monk went to the forest to meditate, worship, and practice yoga. He stayed there for a long time and became a yogi. One day, as he sat under a tree, a few dry leaves fell on his head. Looking up, he saw a crow and a crane fighting in the tree. This angered him, and he glared at them, "Dare you throw leaves on my head?" With his stare a flame of fire flew from his head and burned the birds— such was the yogi's power. The yogi was pleased by his power to burn the crane and crow with just a look.

The yogi later went to town to beg for his bread. He stood at a door and knocked, *Mother, please give me some food.*

Wait a minute, son, said a voice from inside the house.

The yogi thought, *You horrible woman! How dare you make me wait outside your house. You don't know what my power is yet.*

As he thought this, the voice came again, *Boy, don't think so highly of yourself. This woman is neither crow nor crane.*

The yogi was astonished; still he had to wait. At last the woman came outside, and he fell at her feet and said, *Mother, how did you know that?*

She said, *Young boy, I'm just a commoner and I don't know your yoga or your practices. I made you wait because my husband is ill, and I was nursing him. I have struggled all of my life to do my duty. Before I was married, my duty was to my parents, and then after I got married, my duty was to my husband. By doing my duty, I have become illumined, and I could read your thoughts. If you want to progress higher than what you learned in the forest, go to the market in town and seek out a butcher. He'll tell you something that you'll be grateful to learn.*

The young monk thought to himself, *Why would I seek out this butcher?* But after what he had seen, his mind was more open and he went to the market. The butcher was a big, fat man cutting meat with a large and sharp knife while bargaining with several customers.

Am I supposed to learn from this man? the monk wondered.

The butcher noticed the young yogi, *Monk, did the woman send you? Here, sit, while I finish my business.*

The yogi thought, *Why am I here?* but he sat anyway. After the butcher finished his work, he told the monk, *Come, Swami, follow me. Let's go to my home.*

On reaching his home the butcher said *Wait here.* He went into the house, and while the monk waited outside, he gave his old father and mother baths and did what he could to make sure they were comfortable. He then came outside and asked the yogi, *Now, what did you come for?*

How can I help you?

The monk asked him a few questions about soul and God, and the butcher gave him a lecture which forms a part of the Mahabharata, one of the ancient Hindu scriptures. It contains one of the highest episodes of knowing God.

When the butcher finished his teaching, the monk felt astonished. He said, *With such knowledge as yours why are you a butcher, doing such menial work?*

My son, replied the butcher, *no duty is ugly, no duty is impure. My birth placed me in these circumstances. In my boyhood I learned the butcher's trade. I simply try to do my duties to the best of my abilities, including caring for my aged mother and father. I neither know your practices of yoga. Nor have I become a monk. Nevertheless, all that you have heard and seen has come to me through the unattached doing of the duty which belongs to my position.*

Do you understand, Nachiketa?

Yes, Lord.

Listen carefully, Nachiketa, as I reveal the secrets of the law of non-attachment. **Work, but don't form deep impressions**. **Take up big projects, fulfill all your desires and dreams; but in the process of doing so take care not to form such large impressions in** *your mind. The constant seeking of something in pursuit of the goal creates a strong impression which can become a cause for a future desire which will leads to the creation of another dominating impression and so on.*

(Put in a more modern version: When a poor man makes his first fifty thousand dollars it's a grand feeling. However, when the same man goes on to make a million dollars he ends up producing deep impressions in his mind of becoming a multi millionaire. These impressions take the form of an irresistible desire which directs his future course of work. He seems happy but the millionaire experience can't help him grow because he's no longer working out better experiences for himself. The millionaire mind-set has caused a deep impression which can only be fulfilled with the experience of becoming a multi-millionaire.)

After a while, Nachiketa, we don't work. It's the deep impressions formed in our mind which make us work.

So give up this constant seeking of things, Nachiketa. This mad craving of following the footsteps of the countless desires of your mind. **Take up one idea. Make that your life. Think about it. Dream about it and when you have found unity in that idea, then go forward and assert yourself in accomplishing this dream.**

Know this great secret: that the whole of the nature is for your soul and not the soul for the nature. Don't make this mistake of thinking that you've come into the world to work and to help the world. The world doesn't need you. You need the world to work out your experiences.

(Imagine this for a clearer understanding of Yama's explanation. You enter into a gymnasium. There are different machines and weights for a work-out. You pick up a seven pound dumbbell and start exercising. What happens? Your muscles swell. Does the seven pound dumbbell turn to twenty pounds? No. The dumbbell doesn't grow in size. It's your muscles which grow in size. The world is like the gymnasium. It gives you a chance to work out your experiences. Everything that you do in this world is for your own evolution. If you give money to a poor man thinking that by doing so you are helping him you've probably forgotten to thank the poor man for giving you an opportunity to express your sympathy and kindness. You feel good when you give. It's the giver who takes away more than the receiver.)

You must inform your mind that no one in this universe depends on you, Nachiketa. Not one beggar depends on your charity, not one soul on your kindness, not one living on your help. All are helped by nature and will be so helped even though millions of us are not here. The course of nature won't stop for such as you and me. It's only a blessed privilege to you and me that we're allowed in a way to help others to educate ourselves.

This is a great lesson to learn, Nachiketa, and when you've learned it fully you will never be unhappy. You can go and accomplish all your dreams and you'll be a great blessing to this universe. When you've trained your mind and your nerves to realize this idea of the world's non-dependence on you or on anybody there will be no reaction in the form of pain resulting from work. ***You will no longer worry about the results; you will simply have developed the power to get them.***

God doesn't want the world to change. He wants you to evolve. Now, Nachiketa, listen to yet another story.

A poor man who wanted money heard that if he got hold of a ghost he could demand the spirit to bring him money, or anything else he wanted. So this poor man was very eager to find a ghost. He searched for a man who could provide a ghost and finally found a sage with great power. He asked for the sage's help, and the sage asked in return what he would do with a ghost. 'I desire a ghost very much, to work with me, so tell me how to get one.'

The sage responded, 'Don't bother yourself; go home.'

The next day, the poor man went to the sage again, wept and prayed, 'Please give me a ghost, sir, I need one to help me.'

At last the sage, disgusted with the poor man's insistence, said 'Take this charm, repeat this magic word, and a ghost will come. Whatever you tell the ghost to do, he will do. Beware, ghosts are bad spirits and need to be kept busy; otherwise, he'll kill you.'

The poor man noted this and said, 'I can give him work for his entire life.'

The poor man then went into the forest and repeated the magic word over and over. A huge ghost appeared and said, 'I am a ghost and your magic has summoned me here. I will do as you say but you must keep me busy or I'll have to kill you.' The man told the ghost to build him a palace, and the ghost complied. The man then told him, 'Bring me money.' The ghost did so. The man told the ghost, 'Cut down the forest and build a city here.' The ghost said, "It is done. Anything else?"

The poor man now became frightened as he couldn't think of anything else for the ghost to do. The ghost did everything in an instant. The ghost repeated, 'Give me more work, or I'll kill you.' The poor man ran as fast as he could to the sage. 'Sir! Please save my life!' The sage asked the man what the problem was, and the man answered, "I have nothing more to give the ghost. He did everything I said, and in just an instant. Now he's threatening to kill me if I don't give him more work.' Suddenly, the ghost materialized and threatened the poor man in front of the sage, 'I'll eat you now.'

The sage said, 'I'll find a way out. Look at that dog with a curly tail. Draw your sword quickly and cut the tail off and give it to the ghost to straighten out.' The man did so, gave the tail to the ghost, and said

'Straighten out this tail for me.' The ghost slowly straightened it, but as soon as he did, the tail curled up again. The ghost tried again, and again the tail curled up. This went on for days and days until, exhausted, the ghost said, 'I've never had such trouble. I'll make a deal with you. If you let me go, I'll let you keep all I've given you and I won't kill you.'

The poor man gladly accepted the ghost's offer.

This world, Nachiketa, is like the curly tail of a dog. People have been trying to straighten it out for centuries; but, whenever they let go, the tail curls up again. God doesn't want the world to change. He wants you to evolve. You have the potential to work out your experiences, to manifest your true, loving nature. Everything that you do in this world is for your own evolution. So begin by developing the healthy attitude of perfect non-attachment so the results of your actions don't bind you.

Center all your activities on the consciousness of unity (the purusha) and not around the consciousness of individuality (desires of the thinking mind. *When you gain the ability to work* *keeping the force of unity in the background and moving your little self away from the center of all activities, you would have learned the greatest secret of work. That which is led by the consciousness of unity is ever free, timeless, and incapable of being bound by the law of cause and effect When you make this intelligence of unity the center of all activities you break free from the law of karma and the reign of time. The law of cause and effect no longer retains the power to contract or expand your consciousness. You would have mastered the skill to forego the consciousness of invidividuality and lovingly embrace a much higher and powerful consciousness of unity.*

Know this for certain, Nachiketa, that this consciousness of unity was never created and so it can't be bound by the law of cause and effect. The Purusha always existed. There was never a time when it didn't exist. At the end of a life well spent your mind having become free from all desires and filled with the greatness of the spirit of your being will be released from the individual soul (Jiva) will merge into the Purusha- (the soul of unity.

There was never a time when you and I didn't exist, Nachiketa. You know them not I know them all.

Don't grieve over what isn't yours. Strive for the freedom of the soul, which was free but became bound by the law of cause and effect. Work out your karma, place the ideal before you day and night. Out of it will come the power to release you from this illusion of birth and death created by the law of cause and effect. You are ever free and abundant. No force in this universe can exercise control over you. You are the master of this universe, and the creator of your own destiny. Shake off this delusion that you're nothing and embrace the reality of your supremacy. **If you feel weak and powerless, know that this is unbecoming of you. You're here to be and become and not to believe and unbecome.**

Know who you are and strive to become that reality. This becoming of you is your real karma - your search for finding that unity in you. Reject everything unbecoming to you with all your might. Every little thing that lends you power, which leads you towards the goal of unity, embrace with love and affection. Proceed in this direction and you'll be all set to be the next glowing light of the universe.

Don't attempt to fit into nature, Nachiketa. Conquer nature. *Remember that the whole of nature is for the soul and not soul for the nature. The old man must die. You have to let go of your individuality. That tiny speck of individual consciousness which you assumed to be the greatest* and the *only important thing in life is a myth. There are far superior levels of consciousness hidden within this tiny frame of yours which can dazzle this whole universe.*

I'll relate a legend which will help you cast off this ignorance of individuality and embrace the consciousness of unity. This is the story of Indra, the rain god. Indra misbehaved in heaven and was cursed to become a pig on earth. So he had a pig mate and in course of time several little pigs were born to him. He was very happy living with his family, squealing with joy in the mire, forgetting his divine glory and lordship. The other gods in heaven became exceedingly concerned and they came down to earth to beg him to return to heaven as his period of atonement was over.

But Indra would listen to no one and he drove all the gods away. He said, 'I'm very happy here. I have my wife and my family of piglets. Please don't disturb me.'

Seeing no other alternative left the gods destroyed the pig body of Indra. At once Indra regained his divine presence and was surprised to find out that he could have stooped so low to find enjoyment in a pig's body.

So don't fear, Nachiketa, to let go of your individuality. Remember the greatness of the Purusha which is your real nature and willingly let go of your piggish individuality. ***Now listen closely as I reveal to you the greatest secret of how to let go of your individuality.***

The way is not to give up your individuality but to transcend it.

Say to yourself "Through all mouths I speak, With all feet I walk, All minds are mine, The universe is my body, If one leaf may fall how can the tree die? If living in one body gives me so much joy, than living in two would be better, three far better, grander if I can enjoy the whole universe."

The love for individuality is deceiving and unstable but the love for unity is enriching and everlasting. That which is never born and never dies is Purusha and that is your real nature.

Know that Purusha, meditate on that Purusha and strive to be and become that Purusha this should be the goal of every human being on earth..

What dies is the individuality in you, Nachiketa, and not the unity (the Purusha). Know that if it's a fearful thing to die it may be perchance a yet more fearful thing to live long. Always live that death may never find you unprepared.

Concluding so, Yama the lord of death, disappeared and Nachiketa was reunited with his father.

The Spirit of Nachiketa

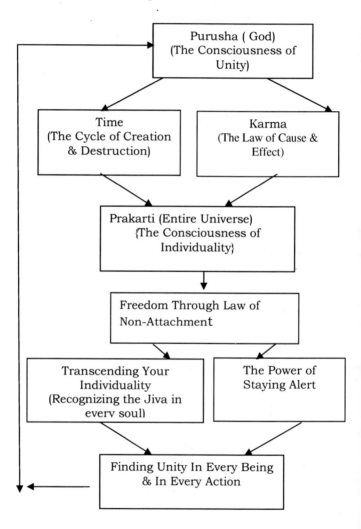

Epilogue

God doesn't exist because death exists.

God exists because love, hatred, crookedness and purity all exist. These seemingly varied forms of human consciousness suggest a unity mankind is moving towards. What makes parents love their children more than others? What is that bond which ties two lovers together? What is it that attracts human beings towards animals and nature? It is the strange relationship of love.

Relationship changes the whole equation of life.

Relationships are the medium which helps us transcend from individuality to unity. Einstein once said: *I want to know God's thoughts; the rest are details.* **Put God before everything. Put unity before individuality and you'll observe that everything falls in place.**

Human beings are divine. We're not machines and our animal nature doesn't represent our true personality. We're endowed with the greatest power to love – to seek unity in all our actions. The future of death and human life lies on the collective consciousness of every individual on this planet and not in the hands of scientists concerned more about prolonging human life. **We have to strive more to expand our consciousness than worry about expanding the duration of our life**. When every individual realizes this unity – 'that one thing' from which everything manifests – human life would have become a grand celebration.

Exercise No 1

How To Fulfill The Biggest Promise You Made To God

Do this exercise before going to sleep. Lie down on the bed on your back with your arms by your sides and your palms facing up. Gently close your eyes and relax your whole body. Breathe very slowly and follow the movement of your breath as you quietly inhale and calmly exhale. Be conscious of the rhythm of your breath as it gradually simmers down with every moment. Enjoy and feel the lightness all over your being. Now silently move your whole consciousness to the big toe on your right leg. As you make this transition imagine a point of light emerging from the core of your being and following your consciousness. This point of light which is luminous circulates your big toe and injects divine energy in every single tissue of your big toe. Revel in this whole celestial experience.

Now move your whole consciousness to the index toe. The moment you make this shift the point of light follows your consciousness and illuminates the whole area of your index toe by circulating it.

Have fun with this whole process. Move your consciousness to all those body parts which you want to light up and watch as this luminous point follows you everywhere. Travel to every part of your body that needs attention and gift it with the divine glow.

Enjoy the whole experience and watch your consciousness jump from one part of the body to another and the divine light accompanying it in all places.

As you continue to play around with your consciousness imagine it takes a big leap and leaves your body. The point of light follows your consciousness and you're now freely moving around in the universe, no longer restricted to the bodily movement. You've achieved freedom from the laws of nature. The law of time and cause and effect no longer have a bearing on you. You're eternally free. You can spend your night on the moon or dance with the stars. You can travel to any place desired in seconds.

While enjoying this freedom you suddenly enter into a dark area in the ecliptic line in the sky. Two celestial beings welcome you here and escort you to their master.

Dressed all in black the master greets you with a cheerful smile, "You have come at the right time. I want to show you something very interesting."

The master then utters a mystical word and you suddenly find your consciousness traveling back in time to the point before your birth. You watch your consciousness guided by the divine intelligence descend from the sky and enter into a grain seed. Over time this seed grows into a food plant and under the supervision of the divine intelligence finds its way into your father's body and is contained in a drop of semen. This semen enters into your mother's womb and on the first night in your mother's womb you watch as the semen containing your consciousness mixes with the ovum to form one unit of the life force called *Kalala*.

Within five days this mixture ferments into a bubble called *Budbuda*. By the tenth day it develops into a small lump of flesh in the shape of a *brinjal* called *Karkura*. In one month this lump containing your consciousness develops into a head and by the end of two months the fingers, toes, hairs bones and genital openings appear. Within four months the seven essential substances of the body – the skin, flesh, blood, bone, fat, marrow and semen or ovum develops. At the end of five months hunger and thirst are felt and by the end of six months your consciousness is covered by a thin membrane called placenta which allows the fetes to move to the right side of the abdomen if your are a male and left side if you are a female. The fetus containing your consciousness grows by receiving nutrition from the food and drink that are consumed by your mother and passed on through the umbilical coɪu.

However, you don't enjoy this whole process as you find your consciousness to be in a very unpleasant place in the midst of all the bodily filth and breeding worms.

Your tender body is bitten all over by these hungry worms and you suffer intensely from the contact of pungent, salty and burning substances eaten by your mother.

As your consciousness goes through this ordeal you also find yourself restricted in your body movements. You remain lying in your mothers womb with your head turned towards your belly such that your back and neck are arched like a bow. You're unable to move your limbs and your consciousness is denied freedom like a bird in a cage. At this moment of intense suffering a point of light which was always invisibly following your consciousness emerges in front of your being and helps you recall your real nature. It reveals to you all your past actions in previous human lives which has became the reason for your consciousness to manifest another human body.

The point of light shows you all the deep impressions and desires of your earlier life times which went unfulfilled, and which became the cause for the law of karma to help you seek another suitable environment to work out those experiences. All the heroic victories and terrible disappointments of your consciousness are flashed before your eyes one after another. The countless, never ending cycle of births and deaths which your consciousness has been revolving under is brought to your attention by this divine light. The journey of your consciousness which once began in a pure and pristine manner but which became caught up in the world of thoughts and senses are laid bare before you.

As the divine light enlightens you on the real nature of your consciousness you remember the true purpose of your existence. *Before the sun, the moon and the earth, before the stars or the comets free long before time was ever born I was, I am and I shall always be.* As you contemplate on this moment of truth your consciousness make a solemn promise to the divine light:

"This human life I will dedicate to knowing and remembering my true divinity. I will not get caught up in the countless desires of my thinking mind and I will direct all my energy to produce actions which lead me to the supreme goal- the Purusha. I will create good karma which over time will wipe out all the cause and effect phenomena of my past actions. I will strive continually to meditate on the highest truth – the true reality of my consciousness"

As you make this resolution the fetus in your mother's womb is pushed out of the womb in the tenth month. Being thus pushed forcefully your consciousness come out of your mother's womb head downwards, breathless and deprived of all memory. Cast amidst blood and urine on the floor your consciousness now finds itself wrapped in a baby body nourished by people who don't understand your needs. From this moment on the world of thoughts and senses gradually begin to influence your consciousness and very soon you again forget your real nature and get caught up in the law of cause and effect. You forget the biggest promise you made to God.

Suddenly you hear a loud sound. Whoosh.... Whoosh.... Your consciousness along with the divine light has reentered into your body and you find yourself sleeping peacefully in the bed.

Exercise No 2

The Three Letters That Can Make You Powerful

Do this exercise on a weekend when you're relaxed. Open a notepad and write on the top of the page "One fine day everything will change in my life."

Divide the page into two and on the right hand side of the page write the letter L on the first line, O on the second line, V on the third line and E on the fourth line. Now write "Love" on the first line on the left hand side of page.

Consciousness of Unity	Consciousness Of Individuality
LOVE	**1) L**
	2) O
	3) V
	4) E

Observe the right hand side of the page. It contains all the letters required to form the word "Love"; yet the individual letters by itself are ignorant of the power of the word love. The consciousness of individuality is always searching and seeking to find the right combination to move towards the consciousness of unity. Everything in this universe is interconnected.

If a tree is cut, if an animal is killed, if an old man dies, your consciousness is affected.

The pain of these events doesn't reach the surface of your consciousness and so you remain ignorant of the connection. There is nothing in the universe which isn't pervaded by the law of unity. Every aspect of the universe is lighted with the background of unity. It's this unity you aspire to reach.

Gently close your eyes and ask yourself "Why should I hate someone?

That whom I am hating and that through which the power of hating developed in me is one and the same.

Understand that this power of hating which has manifested in you through an external event is what you have to destroy. The external event or person is only the suggestion or fact, the power of hating is the real thing- the obstacle in your path to finding the god of unity.

Now close your eyes and sit erect. Breathe slowly. Move your attention from the event or person which was the cause of hatred and bring it to focus on the power of hating brewing impatiently within you. Observe its rapid moments, its erratic fluctuations, and the damage it's causing to the core of your being. Pay close attention as the power of hating destroys the natural rhythm of your breathing and upsets the whole balance of the force of goodness resting in you. Say to yourself:

"I have every right to be angry with an event or person but the ability to hate doesn't befit me. I'm aware that anger and hatred are two separate things.

The cause of my anger could be an external event or person while the cause of hatred is my poor thinking. The power to hate originates from the

core of my being and isn't a good sign for the growth and development of my consciousness. The will to hate has to go...."

Now take a deep breath and let it go. Hold your hands like offering a prayer and chant the sound of Om...Om...Om. When you chant the sound Om... imagine that the sound is originating from your navel. Most of the words that we speak the sound originates from the throat and so the vibrations are felt only around that area. When you chant Om... don't say it like any other word. The sound Om...has to start from your navel around the stomach and its vibration has to be felt in every part of your body.

Always remember that Om...Om.. is a sound and not a word. Enjoy that sound making process of Om...(A U..M) One chant of Om should last for six to eight seconds. After one chanting take a ten second pause and take delight in the calmness permeating your being. Then resume your chanting. In every sitting chant Om either 11 or 27 times.

After chanting open your notepad and cross out the right hand side of the page

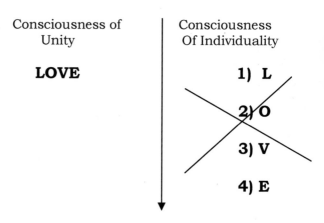

Consciousness of Unity

Consciousness Of Individuality

LOVE

1) **L**
2) **O**
3) **V**
4) **E**

Open a new page and write:

"The will to hate and the will to love both originate from the core of my being. One destroys while other heals. I will strive to conduct my life with the power of the mighty spirit that is within me, unattached, full of love and hope, complete with the strength and divinity manifested by all the great men and women. To love is to live and to hate is to die. Let us all love each other if we can.

Exercise No 3

You will not die on Dec 21st 2012

Imagine that it is Dec 19th 2012. You go to bed at night and you don't get up in the morning of Dec 20th 2012. Imagine you're now declared dead. How would your death be different from the 7 billion people who are estimated to die on Dec 21st 2012? Death is death, period. Aren't the lives of all those people who are dying everyday and who will continue to die before Dec 21st 2012 important? Every human life in this planet is precious. This is the greatest truth. You can never die because you were never born. That which dies isn't worthy to be mourned.

Remember that nightmares always begin pleasantly; only at the worst point the dream is broken. So death breaks the dream of life. Love death. Meditate on death.

Now close your eyes, sit erect and meditate on that which dies with death. Recall the countless cycles of birth and death which you've endured. The million of bodies your consciousnesses have entered into continuously struggling to reach the summit of truth- the consciousnesses of unity. How can your desires die with the death of your body? How can your mind be destroyed when it has experiences yet to be fulfilled? How can your individual consciousness be smashed to pieces until it has merged with the God of unity?

Say to yourself:

"I have died a million times before. Death is not a stranger to me. That which has died a million times I do not consider it worthy to be mourned. I have a task before me. To live life in its fullest and purest form. **Happiness and struggle is the motto of my life. I am convinced that there can be no happiness without struggle**. When it was all dark and when life was passing out of me I used to say struggle... struggle... When light was breaking in and new life was created I still said struggle struggle. I am not afraid of that infinite starry vault that is waiting to crush me for I am aware that in few hours the whole of it would be under my feet..."

Rest a moment, then continue:

Death is divine. Life is divine. **That which I fear in death is the struggle of my individual consciousness to embrace the supreme consciousness**. I can never die. There is no power in this earth or beyond that can destroy me. That which fire cannot burn, the wind cannot dry, the water cannot wet I am that force- that force that love that magic exists in me and I in that force....

Now chant the following Sanskrit mantra 11 times. This mantra has helped millions of people to conquer the death of the individual consciousness and embrace the divinity of the supreme consciousness.

OM... Tryambakam yajamahe
Sugandhim pushti-vardhanam

Urvarukamiva bandhanan
Mrityor mukshiya mamritat

The meaning of the mantra is:

I worship the supreme consciousness who is fragrant in nature and nourishes and grows all beings. As the ripened cucumber is liberated from its bondage to the creeper may He who dwells in us liberate us from the death of the individual consciousness

and give us the strength to embrace the
supreme being

Note: Most of the fruits when it is ripened
falls off the tree to the ground but
cucumber is the only fruit which doesn't
not fall off the tree on its own. It requires
the intervention of the farmer. If the farmer
doesn't pluck it the cucumber rots .
Similarly, the human mind - no matter how
spiritually evolved it is – doesn't give way
to a far superior force waiting to embrace
it. It acts as an obstacle to its own growth.
The above mantra is the prayer to the
supreme being to intervene and enable you
to severe the connection to your thinking
mind and dwell on the glory of the great
spirit.

Exercise No 4

A Simple Technique To Know The Beginning of the Universe

Do this exercise in the weekend. Imagine that you have a desire to eat some tasty food and you decide to cook it yourself. Let's say you decided to cook a pizza. You preheat the oven and make the pizza on a pizza pan and put it in the oven for about 15 minutes. After 15 minutes your pizza is ready. You then spice it up with your favorite toppings and you're all set to enjoy the pizza with your family.

Now take a notepad and divide the page into two. On the right hand side of the page write "The Beginning and End of Pizza" and on the left hand side write "Idea of Pizza."

Record the date and time when you started making the pizza and also note the time when you and your family had finished eating the pizza. (For the sake of example let's choose a date of March 24 and any random time.

Idea of Pizza	The Beginning & End Of Pizza
	Date: 24ᵗʰ March 2010
	a) Start of the Pizza: 10.30am
	b) End of the Pizza 11.15am

Now ask yourself this question:

"When I had finished eating up the last piece of pizza what really came to an end? There was no more pizza in the plate as it was sitting lazily inside my stomach but there was something related to the pizza which continued to exist even after I had gobbled up the last piece of the pizza.

The idea of the pizza continues to exist even after the pizza ceases to exist. It is this idea that becomes the cause for a future desire in my mind to cook and eat another pizza.

Let's assume after three days you again get the desire to cook and eat a pizza. You repeat the same process and enjoy eating the pizza with your family. Take your notepad again and record the timing when you started making the pizza and also note the time when you finished eating the pizza.

Idea of Pizza	The Beginning & End Of Pizza
	Date: 27ʰ March 2010
	a) Start of the Pizza: 6.00 pm
	b) End of the Pizza 7.30 pm

Now if someone asks you:

"When did you first start making the pizza?"

What would you answer? You might answer:

"The first time I made it on 24th March 2010. I started cooking it at 10.30 am and by 11.15 am we had finished eating the pizza. The second time I made it on 27th March 2010.. I started cooking at 6.00 pm and finished eating it at 7.30 pm. and so on..."

Is your answer completely true? Not really.

A pizza cannot be made without an idea of the pizza already existing.

This idea of the pizza existed before you started making the first pizza and continued to exist even after you had finished eating up the last pizza. The idea of the pizza never dies. It always existed. You might not have been aware of this idea before but it always existed, waiting to manifest itself. This manifestation in the form of a tasty pizza has a beginning and an end but this beginning and end doesn't mean the start and end of the idea of the pizza. The idea of a pizza always existed and will continue to exist in the future and will become the cause and reason for more pizzas to be cooked in the future.

Now take a new page divide the page into two and write the "Idea of the universe" on the left hand side and "Beginning and End of the universe" on the right hand side. .

Idea of the universe | **Beginning & End Of the Universe**

Now ask yourself the question: *"When did the universe begin?"*

The word 'beginning' is misleading. It forces you to think that everything must have a start and end.

But that isn't true. The start and end is only of the gross form but there is something which is finer and beyond the gross which is the mother of all causes which continues to exist even after the destruction of the gross form. The sun, the moon, the oceans, human beings, animals, plants everything that you see created in this universe has a beginning and will have an end; but there is something beyond all these gross objects which doesn't have a beginning and will never have an end.

Try this simple exercise. Try to create anything which never existed before. It is impossible. Everything that is created in this world has to exist in some fine form before.

You can't create something which didn't exist earlier.

Read this a hundred times. The sun, the moon, the oceans, human beings, animals, plants everything that you see created in this universe had to exist before in some form. This form is represented as the cosmic intelligence (idea of the universe) from which the whole universe manifested. If you now ask what is the source of this cosmic intelligence we can never come to the conclusion because one source would lead to another and so on. So for simplicity sake cosmic intelligence 'is considered to be the mother of all sources. This source enjoys certain characteristics. It has an independent existence incapable of being acted upon by anything. There is no force superior to it. This intelligence or force can never be destroyed because it was never created.

Creation, it should be noted is not an addition of things; it is always a projection of things which already existed.

Everything that is projected from this cosmic intelligence has a beginning and an end but this intelligence which is the source of all projection in the universe doesn't have a beginning and an end. There was never a time when it did not exist.

So the real answer to the question: When the universe began is this:

The idea of the universe represented by the cosmic intelligence never had a beginning and will never have an end.

Everything that is projected from this cosmic intelligence has a beginning and an end. This beginning and end is called one life cycle of the universe. At the end of one life cycle the universe is destroyed and it returns back to its source. There it exists as the idea of the universe which becomes the cause for another projection of the universe in the form of another life cycle and so on....

Now close your eyes and meditate on that one reality from which everything else manifests and into which everything returns back.

(Readers are requested to read the chapters "The source of all intelligence" from my earlier book "Know that one thing" which I have reproduced at the end of the book in the form of an appendix which will help you gain more clarity on the characteristics of the cosmic intelligence.)

Exercise No 5

How to light up your whole day with a simple 12 minute breathing exercise

You can do this exercise anytime in the morning before your breakfast or in the evening before your dinner. Sit down comfortably in a quiet place. Sit erect holding the head, shoulders and hips in a straight line keeping the spinal column free. The spinal column is our main working ground on which all the subtle movements surrounding our breathing will happen, so it is important that the spine is kept free.

Gently close your eyes and relax. Now close the right nostril with the thumb and slowly inhale through the left nostril. As you inhale mentally focus on the sound Om. Repeat the sound Om four times to complete one inhalation. Now close your left nostril with the index finger such that both your nostrils are now closed and hold the breath in. This act of retention of the breath is the most important part of this breathing exercise. As you hold the breath mentally focus on the sound OM eight times.

Every time that you repeat Om forcefully imagine throwing this restrained breath at the base of the spine.

The base of the spine is the place where all divine energy is resting latently. Our task is to arouse and awaken it. By forcibly imagining throwing this restrained breath at the base of the spine we express our willingness and desire to align our activities with this supreme force. Now remove the thumb from the right nostril exhale slowly through it repeating Om four times. As you close the exhalation draw in the abdomen forcibly inside to expel all the air from the lungs.

There are three steps to this breathing exercise. Inhaling, Retention and exhaling. Inhale to a count of 4 times retain the breath to a count of 8 times and exhale to a count of 4 times again.

Now repeat the same process inhaling through the right nostril. Keep the left nostril closed using the index finger and inhale through the right nostril mentally repeating Om four times. Next close the right nostril with the thumb and hold the breath mentally focusing on the sound of OM eight times. As you retain this breath imagine throwing this restrained breath forcibly at the base of the spine to awaken the divine energy. Then unclose the left nostril and slowly exhale through the left nostril repeating Om four times drawing in the abdomen as before.

This breathing exercise is called *Pranayam*. At every sitting do four such rounds of breathing. Breathing has the ability to make a significant impact on your thinking process. As you progress in this direction you would have developed the uncanny ability to watch your thoughts coming from a distance just as you could look out and see a person coming from a distance. Your thoughts will announce their coming and you'll be able to identify the root cause of these thoughts and deal with them in the right manner. You'll gain greater insight into the world of thoughts and will master the skill to either ride along or step aside from these thoughts. As you develop in this path you'll be able to discriminate between a thought, the feelings associated with the thought, and the present moment. You would havelearned the skill to disassociate your consciousness from the thought world and begin a new way of being.

- -

Be cheerful, be brave, bathe daily, have patience, purity and perseverance while doing Pranayama. You will then become a Yogi in truth. Never try to hurry, and if the higher powers come remember that they are but side-paths. Do not let them tempt you from the main road, put them aside and hold fast to your only true aim- God. Seek only the Eternal, finding which we are at rest for ever, having the all, nothing is left to strive for, and we are forever in free and perfect existence- Existence absolute, Knowledge absolute, Bliss absolute.

Swami Vivekananda

****

Exercise No 6

God is selfish. Is this true? Find out for yourself in less than seven seconds....

Imagine God is in a dilemma. In the next two seconds something horrible is going to happen. He needs your help in finding a solution. He wants you to go through the list of future events below and suggest him a suitable line of action.

a) A group of terrorists are about to blow a major five star hotel in
Mumbai. 844 people are expected to die in this tragedy

b) A wicked man is about to rape a 21 year old women.

c) A thief is about to steal the life savings of an old man who just returned home after withdrawing money from the bank

d) A pure man who has led a life of integrity and honesty is about to commit a crooked act.

e) Three teenagers are about to get together and plan an evil act for the first time in their life

f) Your child who is crossing the road this moment is about to be hit and killed by a drunken truck driver.

All the events above are expected to take place in the next two seconds. If you had one second to react which event will you avert?

You would obviously save your child. Well that is not what God might have done. Infact it could be possible that he might not have interfered with any of these horrible events above. One of the important things that you have got to realize before you point fingers at the intelligence of God is : **Your order of importance in dealing with the issues of the world is quite selfish as can be seen from your choice in the above example**. Human beings can only see the world through them, they do not have the ability to observe the world as it is.

God does not carry any emotions. It is important that you understand this. If he did he would never have allowed any bad event to take place on earth. God is all intelligence. This intelligence can never falter. Never that is the word. Our minds are too small to think beyond the realm of our desires. God doesn't have the power to undo a human act. He doesn't even attempt to do that. He only gives you a better opportunity to grow...

Exercise 7

Look who is watching all your actions!

Imagine this short story before going to bed every day.

Long long ago there lived a pious sage called Vishwamitra in the southern part of India. During those days there were no formal schools and parents used to send their children to wise sages to learn and imbibe the highest aspects of life. The children used to stay permanently with these sages for twelve years after which they would return back to their parents. Narendra was one such child who studied under the guidance of the sage Vishwamitra.

At the end of twelve years the sage Vishwamitra conducted a final test to measure the progress of each child. He gave every child a unique activity depending on their personality. Narendra was very sharp and intelligent and Vishwamtira wanted to give his best student the toughest exercise.

He called Narendra close to him and said:

Naren, you have been a wonderful student. Today is the last day of your stay here and I want you to succeed in an important task."

The sage handed Narendra a small dove and a knife. Take this dove to a remote place where no one is watching and kill it. After you have killed the dove bring it back to me. Take care that no one should watch you when you kill the dove.

Narendra was puzzled. In his twelve years with the sage he had always been instructed not to harm innocent beings. How could he kill a gentle dove! But he had no choice. He had to carry out the instructions of his guru and so he left for a remote place...

Everywhere that he went he found someone watching him. He then entered deep into a forest. There was not a single human being there. As he was about to kill the dove a thought came to his mind that there are no human beings here but there are other birds and animals watching his actions. Fearing that he would fail in his test he entered further deep into the forest and came to a place where there wasn't a single soul. No human beings, no birds, no animals.

As Narendra prepared himself to kill the dove another thought raced across his mind --- There are no human beings here. There are no animals and birds here. Does that mean my actions will go unrecorded? Who will be the witness to his horrifying act that I am about to commit?

As these thoughts took possession of him a strange power manifested from the core of his being instructing Narendra to calm down and feel at ease. In the middle of the forest Narendra sat down in deep meditation holding the gentle dove in his right hand.

A divine glow had spread all over his face. A voice from within spoke:

Naren.. You are the sole witness of every activity. Every action of yours is recorded in the form of an impression in your consciousness. No action can escape the law of karma- the law of cause and effect. There is no place in this world where the Purusha (the divine intelligence) does not exist. ***You are the doer and you are the sole witness. The former is the***

individual consciousness in you and the latter the divine. *Your task is to produce actions on the individual plane of consciousness that befit the supreme being working in the background for you. Get up, Naren, and hand over the dove back to your master.*

Holding the dove Naren ran back as fast he could to his master. With mixed emotions of fear and joy he narrated the sequence of events to Vishwamitra. He feared that he might have failed in his final test but the joy of having discovered the greatest truth kept him cheerful. Vishwamitra embraced the little child and blessed him.

Narendra, you have passed the final test and made me proud. You have realized the greatest secret of existence. The creator, the created and the method of creation are all identical. That one thing is eternal and pervasive. It is present in every action. No action can escape the law of karma- the law of cause and effect. You are the doer and you are the sole witness.

Vishwamitra blessed Narendra and instructed him to release the dove.

Narendra kissed the gentle dove and let it go....

****

The Supreme Self, smaller than the smallest, and greater than the greatest, lies concealed in the heart of all creatures. Know him to be all pervasive and immortal. The Supreme Being can't be attained by study of scriptures or by intellect and vast learning. It is gained by him alone who wholeheartedly seeks for it. To such an aspirant the Self reveals its own nature.

Katha Upanishad

****

Appendix A

How can we know that there is something behind this mind and body?

Let's understand this with a more simple example. Take a look at the computer. How could the computer have come into existence? There is only one way: **Thru intelligence.**

So where is the intelligence stored in the computer?

    a)   In the Monitor
    b)   In the keyboard
    c)   In the CPU(Central Processing Unit)

We all know that the monitor and the keyboard don't carry that intelligence. Its utility is restricted to viewing and typing. The real intelligence which runs the computer is stored in a small chipset in the CPU. However, we also know that the intelligence of the CPU is limited and that there is intelligence beyond the CPU.

How do we know that? Because it a human brain which developed the CPU! The computer doesn't have the understanding that there is something beyond itself because all its functions are executed technologically. In a similar manner human beings fail to understand that there is something beyond the mind because most of the activities of our daily life are met and executed through the workings of our regular thought processes. But just as we know that there is intelligence beyond the CPU we can also find out there is a intelligence beyond our body and mind if we examine the source of all our knowledge.

PROOF

Intelligence can't belong to the human body

How do our fingers move, our legs walk, our eyes see, our ears hear? What is the source of intelligence of the human body? Intelligence can't belong to dead or dull matter. Never was seen any gross matter which had intelligence as its own essence. No dull or dead matter can illumine itself. The body can't be the source of its own intelligence. Its intelligence must have been borrowed from something else. We saw in the earlier example that the intelligence of the monitor and keyboard is borrowed from the CPU. Similarly, the intelligence of the body is **borrowed** from the human mind.

However, just as the intelligence of the CPU is borrowed from the human mind, which is higher than the CPU, the intelligence of the human mind is borrowed from something higher. How can we know this?

Intelligence can't belong to the human mind

We saw earlier that the moon waxes and wanes because its light is borrowed from the Sun. If a lump of iron is put into the fire and made red-hot it glows and shines but its light will vanish because it is borrowed. **So decadence is possible only of that light which is borrowed and is not of its own essence.** The human mind is vigorous at one time and weak at another because it can be acted upon by anything and everything. Therefore the light which shines through the mind is not its own.

Anything which is subject to change and which can be acted upon can't be the source of its own intelligence. Accordingly, the human mind can't be the source of its own intelligence. Its intelligence must have been **borrowed** from something else.

So what is the source of this infinite human intelligence?

****

Whose is it then? It must belong to that which has it as its own essence, and as such can never decay or die, never become stronger or weaker, it is self – luminous, it is luminosity itself. **That which is happy has borrowed its happiness, that which has knowledge has received its knowledge and that which has a relative existence has only a reflected existence.** Wherever there are qualities, these qualities have been reflected upon the substance, but "that one thing" has not knowledge, existence and blessedness as its qualities, they are the **essence** of "that one thing".

Swami Vivekananda

****

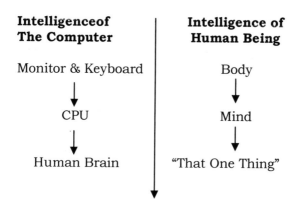

Intelligenceof The Computer	Intelligence of Human Being
Monitor & Keyboard	Body
↓	↓
CPU	Mind
↓	↓
Human Brain	"That One Thing"

THAT ONE THING

Let's take a closer look at "that one thing" which is higher than the mind and the body.

We can only know "that one thing" by defining its characteristics which must be superior than the mind and the body. So let's define its uniqueness:

a) If "that one thing'" can't decay or die like the human body then it can **never be destroyed**. It is eternal and everlasting.

b) If "that one thing" can never be subject to change like the human mind it means

it cannot be acted upon by anything. There is no force superior to it which can influence its behavior.

c) If "that one thing" can't borrow its intelligence **it means it should have an independent existence.** It can't be the outcome of anything. It always existed. There was never a time when it did not exist.

d) If "that one thing" should have an independent existence it means it cannot have a relative existence. If it can't have a relative existence it means **it should have an absolute existence**.

It can't be that the sun has light but *it is* light. *Light isn't a quality of the sun but it is its core essence and so the light of the sun is absolute*. However, when the same light of the sun falls upon any object the light is no longer absolute in relation to that object. It becomes relative because the light is borrowed and light is seen more as a quality of that object. So wherever you see qualities in an object it has a relative existence. "That one thing" should be absolute.

To reiterate: that which is happy has borrowed its happiness, that which has knowledge has received its knowledge, and that which has a relative existence has only a reflected existence. Wherever there are qualities, these qualities have been reflected upon the substance, but "that one thing" hasn't knowledge, existence and blessedness as its qualities; they are the essence of "that one thing."

It can't be "that one thing" knows; *it is* knowledge. It can't be "that one thing" has existence; *it is* existence. It can't be "that one thing" is happy; *it is* happiness itself.

All the qualities of happiness, knowledge, existence found within us are not the qualities of "that one thing" - they are its core essence!

Notice four distinct characteristics of "that one thing" which are the source of all human intelligence.

1) "That one thing" can never be destroyed
2) "That one thing" can never be acted upon by anything
3) "That one thing" has independent existence
4) "That one thing" has absolute existence

Appendix B

Purusha – God, universal soul, consciousness of unity

Jiva - individual soul

Prakarti – cosmic intelligence, consciousness of individuality.

Prana- life force

Panchang- science of perfect timing

Karma- law of cause and effect